I Ride

Katie Peters

GRL Consultant Diane Craig,
Certified Literacy Specialist

Lerner Publications ◆ Minneapolis

Note from a GRL Consultant
This Pull Ahead leveled book has been carefully designed for beginning readers.
A team of guided reading literacy experts has reviewed and leveled the book to
ensure readers pull ahead and experience success.

Lerner Publications
An imprint of Lerner Publishing Group, Inc.
241 First Avenue North
Minneapolis, MN 55401 USA

For reading levels and more information, look up this title at www.lernerbooks.com.

Main body text set in Memphis Pro 24/39
Typeface provided by Linotype.

Photo Acknowledgments
The images in this book are used with the permission of: © suprun/iStockphoto, p. 3;
© Marilyn Nieves/iStockphoto, pp. 4–5; © RonTech2000/iStockphoto, pp. 6–7, 16
(van); © Monkey Business Images/Shutterstock Images, pp. 8–9, 16 (bus); © ArtMarie/
iStockphoto, pp. 10–11; © Imgorthand/iStockphoto, pp. 12–13; © Zinkevych/iStockphoto,
pp. 14–15, 16 (boat).

Front cover: © SolStock/iStockphoto

Library of Congress Cataloging-in-Publication Data

Names: Peters, Katie, author.
Title: I ride / Katie Peters.
Description: Minneapolis, MN : Lerner Publications, [2023] | Series: My world (pull ahead readers
 - nonfiction) | Includes index. | Audience: Ages 4–7 | Audience: Grades K–1 | Summary:
 "Carefully leveled text and full-color photographs invite readers to explore the types of
 transportation people use. Pairs with the fiction book From the Train"— Provided by publisher.
Identifiers: LCCN 2022006355 (print) | LCCN 2022006356 (ebook) | ISBN 9781728475998
 (library binding) | ISBN 9781728478913 (paperback) | ISBN 9781728483825 (ebook)
Subjects: LCSH: Transportation—Juvenile literature. | Choice of transportation—Juvenile
 literature.
Classification: LCC HE152 .P45 2023 (print) | LCC HE152 (ebook) | DDC 388—dc23/eng/20220217

LC record available at https://lccn.loc.gov/2022006355
LC ebook record available at https://lccn.loc.gov/2022006356

Manufactured in the United States of America
1 – CG – 12/15/22

Table of Contents

I Ride

I ride in a car.

I ride in a van.

I ride in a bus.

I ride in a train.

I ride in a plane.

I ride in a boat.

What type of transportation do you use the most?

Did You See It?

boat

bus

van

Index